Written by Lisa Ne[wby]

INTRODU[CTION]

In the early days of its existence in England, [smuggling was] exportation rather than importation, and was directly concerned with the wool trade, England's main industry during the medieval era. The export of raw wool was prohibited by the Government in an attempt to protect the home-weaving industry from its European rivals. While the weavers benefited from this measure, the wool-growers found that they were unable to ask high prices for their crop owing to lack of competition. Thus, they were forced to export wool illegally in order to make a profit. These original wool smugglers were known as 'Owlers' (because they worked by night) and they operated mainly from Kent and Sussex. Import smuggling as we know it grew up when customs dues were first introduced. The customs system was created by Edward I in 1272 to help finance the wars against France but no preventive system was established till 1421, and even then it was negligible. Meanwhile, smuggling had been growing into an organised operation with nothing to hinder it, for it was, after all, only a minor problem compared with England's succession of wars, and no men were available at that time to suppress it.

As new duties were levied on tobacco, tea, brandy, rum, silks, muslins, hand-kerchiefs and even salt they became targets for smugglers. There was more smuggling in Devon and Cornwall than anywhere else in England – it was once estimated that, if all the goods smuggled into Falmouth alone in the course of one year had been taxed, the money collected would have been more than twice the land tax for the whole kingdom – and its character was noticeably different

Smugglers running spirits, 1807

from that of the other smuggling regions. The West Country smugglers tended to be less violent, preferring to use their natural cunning; smugglers elsewhere would without hesitation murder anyone who stood in their way.

Smuggling was a way of life to the poverty-stricken inhabitants of Devon and Cornwall. They lived by the coast, surrounded by secret landing-places and smuggling to them was just a logical extension of the fishing trade. They held the Government's customs duties in the greatest contempt: 'But why should the King tax good liquor? If they must have taxes, why can't they tax something else?' Also, since they had paid for the contraband goods in the first place, they failed to see why their actions should be regarded as criminal.

The famous eighteenth-century economist Adam Smith defined a smuggler (or a 'Fair Trader' as they preferred to call themselves) as: 'A person who, though no doubt highly blamable for violating the laws of his country, is frequently incapable of violating those of natural justice and who would have been in every respect an excellent citizen had not the laws of his country made that a crime which Nature never meant to be so.' This was such a widespread attitude in Devon and Cornwall that everyone, from the fisherman to the magistrate and even the parson, took part in the proceedings.

This allegiance was beneficial to all the community, for smuggling could not exist without loyalty, while all those concerned were generously rewarded. The Reverend R. S. Hawker, vicar of the Cornish parish of Morwenstow, relates this revealing tale of an honest traveller who comes upon a group of smugglers landing a cargo in a little cove. Disgusted, he shouts: "What a horrible sight! Have you no shame? Is there no magistrate at hand? Cannot any Justice of the Peace be found in this fearful country?" "No – thanks be to God," answered a hoarse, gruff voice, "none within eight miles." "Well, then," screamed the stranger, "Is there no clergyman hereabout? Does no minister of the parish live among you on this coast?" "Aye! to be sure there is," said the same deep voice. "Well, how far off does he live? Where is he?" "That's he yonder, Sir, with the lanthorn." And sure enough, there he stood on a rock and poured,

Below: *The sun dispelling a mist with smugglers landing their cargo,* an engraving from a painting by H.R. Parkes, 1851
Right: *The Smuggler's intrusion,* engraved from a painting by Sir David Wilkie R.A.

Left: *Smugglers attacked by revenue men, c.* 1820
Below: *Halt smugglers* by H.P. Parker

with pastoral diligence, the light of other days on a busy congregation.' The parsons were not always so amenable but it was rare indeed to find any taking the part of the exciseman, for smugglers provided a necessary service to the community, supplying everyone with the little luxuries of life at a price even the poorest could afford.

Even the revenue men or gaugers themselves (they gauged the amount of duty payable) were not above reproach and could be bribed, using, for instance a 'gauger's pocket', a concealed fissure or deep crack in the cliff face, over which a stone could be placed and into which a bag of gold could be dropped to ensure the absence of the officer when contraband was being run ashore.

While smuggling was not the glamorous and romantic adventure that we like to imagine, it was certainly a recognised, even respected, profession through which the majority of the population gained a better standard of living.

SMUGGLER'S HAUNTS IN CORNWALL

Cawsand, a typical Cornish smuggling village

Cawsand may perhaps be described as a typical Cornish smuggling village; indeed, Commander H. N. Shore wrote of it: 'When the final history of Cornish smuggling comes to be written, the place of honour will probably be awarded to Cawsand.' The village was ideal in many ways, for it was close to the great contraband market of Plymouth and yet it was small enough to possess rambling alleyways, nooks and crannies where the goods could be hidden if necessary. Moreover, the small boats used here for fishing were also well suited for smuggling. A contemporary writer describes this amusing scene at Cawsand: 'In going down the hill, towards Kingsand, we met several females, whose appearance was so grotesque and extraordinary, that I could not imagine in what manner they had contrived to alter their natural shapes so completely, till, upon enquiry, we found that they were smugglers of spirituous liquors; which they were at that time conveying from their cutter at Plymouth by means of bladders fastened under their

petticoats; and indeed, they were so heavily laden, that it was with great apparent difficulty they waddled along . . . the principal annoyances to these "honest" traders is their intercourse with drunken sailors . . . it is not infrequently that these jolly sons of Neptune pierce the bladders with their knives and highly enjoy the confusion they have occasioned.'

Smuggling was by no means confined to secluded coves; it also flourished in larger harbours such as Looe. Looe Island, just off the coast, was once the home of two unusually violent smugglers, Fyn and his sister, Black Joan. At first a negro lived with them but he was soon murdered and thereafter his ghost haunted the beach. Black Joan and Fyn apparently also cleared the island of rodents by eating them! Yet despite these atrocities, the couple proved very useful to the smugglers of Looe. The contact man on the mainland was a farmer, who often used to ride his distinctive white horse to market. 'If the white horse were seen returning along the coast road to the west, that was a signal to Fyn that all was safe. But sometimes the horse was too lame or tired to return home and the farmer went his way on foot. That always coincided with activity among the officers of the revenue. From Looe Island, Fyn signalled by lights to the smugglers lying in the offing.'

Equally notorious was Polperro, which specialised in building fast and well-armed vessels capable of out-running the excisemen. One such lugger, the *Unity,* made 500 successful trips before she was captured. The entire population of Polperro took part in smuggling and when one of them, Roger Toms, turned informer, they took the law into their own hands and kidnapped him. Eventually, Polperro's nefarious activities so angered the authorities that one of the first resident excise units was established here in the 1800s. The unfortunate officials, however, were forced to live in an abandoned boat as no villager would give them lodgings!

Near Polperro were two favourite smugglers' haunts: the eerie Talland churchyard, which was conveniently 'haunted' by 'devils' (who bore a strong resemblance to the local villains!), and the picturesque Punch Bowl Inn at Lanreath, where the fair-traders would gather to distribute their goods.

Fowey, a little further along the coast, was proud of the title 'Fowey Gallants' that its seafaring men had earned during the Siege of Calais in 1346 when they harassed the French coast with piratical raids. There was still a touch of the pirate in the Fowey smugglers, which led to some violent clashes with the excisemen.

Below: East and West Looe (print of 1832)
Right: Polperro

One of the most notable smugglers here was Richard Kingcup, who started his career as a revenue officer, but: 'He was too sharp for the coastguard and, as he couldn't get his promotion, he chucked it and set up a public house on the quay called the Crown and Anchor . . . he took to smuggling reg'lar then, a proper busy fellow he was.'

Mevagissey, another port with ancient origins, grew rich on its pilchard-fishing and smuggling. It specialised in building fast ships (some could cross the Channel in eight hours if the wind was favourable) which were used by smugglers all over Cornwall.

Falmouth, one of the finest natural harbours in the world, probably owes its very existence to smuggling, for it was developed both as a town and a harbour in the sixteenth century by the Killigrews, a rich and influential family whose money came from piracy and smuggling. Sir John Killigrew who, ironically, held the position of Vice-Admiral of Cornwall, originally merely invested in or received the goods, but eventually he began to lead the raiding expeditions himself. All the

Top left: Fowey (print of 1860)
Bottom left: the Punch Bowl Inn, Lanreath
Top right: *Sailors attacking smugglers* (woodcut
c. 1812)
Bottom right: the port of Mevagissey

family took part in these bloodthirsty forays, including Lady Killigrew, who was suspected of drowning several crew-members of a Spanish ship that she wanted to loot. Although the seat of the Killigrews was at Arwenacke, Falmouth (contraband was stored in the mansion while Lady Killigrew sometimes buried her booty in the garden), most of their raids were carried out on the Helford River, where they owned all the harbours. Thus, since they used only their own private and well-guarded harbours to unload their contraband, they were in no danger from the excisemen.

The Falmouth excisemen were in league with the smugglers anyway, so hardly any seizures were made here – in fact, the Falmouth Customs House was built by the Killigrews! On the few occasions when the excise-men were active, the smugglers would simply carry on around the coast to the secluded haven of Mullion Cove, and unload there. Sometimes, Indiamen would anchor in Falmouth harbour for several weeks, selling their contraband goods quite openly. One contemporary writer remarked: 'It is thought that there are not less than 20,000 pounds worth of such things left among us

from the three last ships. The Captains and officers are allowed large privileges and there are ways and means of dealing with custom-house officers well known to those who deal in Uncustomed Goods.'

In 1688, Falmouth was appointed a Packet Port for the mail boats, thus opening up great smuggling opportunities with Lisbon. Again, we are told: 'The Captains themselves smuggle large quantities and connive at the men doing the same, not allowing them sufficient wages whereon to live without it.' Unfortu-nately for them, this liberal way of life came to an abrupt end in the eighteenth century when an honest man, Samuel Pellew, was appointed Collector of Customs here, and 'took the most active measures to give efficiency to his office'. It has been said that all ranks engaged in smuggling; indeed one Philip Hawkins, MP for Grampound, some miles upriver from Falmouth, is reputed to have left £600 to the King as 'conscience' money.

Many fine tales of smuggling around The Lizard are told. On more than one occasion a well-intentioned revenue man would invite (or perhaps coerce would be a better term) a group of known smugglers to act as a 'jury' in determining the contents of casks 'washed up' on a beach. If they agreed the casks contained spirits, he

Below: Falmouth
Opposite: (top) the River Helford; (bottom) Mullion Cove

proposed to seize them 'in the Queen's name'; if they contained sea-water he would break them open and pour the contents out. If, however, they contained spirits 'affected by sea-water in the opinion of the jury' the casks would be available for removal and the contents for disposal by the 'jury' and so honour was satisfied.

The most renowned of all Cornwall's smugglers were the Carter family: eight brothers and two sisters, of whom the most influential figures were John, the eldest son, and his brothers Harry and Charles. John earned his nickname, 'the King of Prussia', in his boyhood days, when he called himself 'the King of Prussia' (as Frederick the Great was commonly known) whilst playing at soldiers. The name stuck so fast that even the cove where they set up their headquarters, originally called Porth Leah, was dubbed 'Prussia Cove'.

Prussia Cove was actually made up of two inlets – one known as 'Bessie's Cove' after the landlady of the 'kidleywink' (inn) there – separated by rocks. Situated in Mounts Bay, this was an ideal spot from which to carry out smuggling operations, for it was completely protected from prying eyes by its overhanging cliffs and steep, rocky sides which could only be negotiated by tortuous pathways. Moreover, it was riddled with caves, somes of which connected by secret passages to the Carters' house on the cliff top. Just as an extra precaution, the 'King' set up a battery of small cannon on the cliffs (ostensibly as a protection from French privateers), which were actually fired one day when the revenue cutter *Fairy* misguidedly ventured too near. It is unlikely that this harsh reception was intended to cause any real damage: the cutter left hastily but unharmed while only a half-hearted attempt at retaliation was made the next day by a troop of soldiers.

John Carter was a man of strict integrity, the epitome of the 'honest smuggler', and respected by everyone who

knew him, even the revenue men, as the following anecdote illustrates. The Carters being away on business one day, the customs officers from Penzance took the opportunity to search the house and secured a considerable cargo of tea and brandy which was removed to the Penzance customs house. On his return, the 'King' was not so much concerned with the actual loss of his goods as with disappointing his customers, most of whom had already paid, and breaking his promise to deliver the goods. Thus, the Carters went to Penzance in the dead of night, broke into the customs house and removed their captured goods. When the theft was discovered in the morning, the excisemen at once identified their culprit – 'John Carter has been here, and

Left: Prussia Cove
Above: Penzance
Below: Harry Carter

Print of Penzance

we know it because he is an upright man and has taken away nothing which was not his own.'

While John Carter prided himself on his strict code of honour, his brother Henry (Captain Harry) suffered from so many pangs of conscience that he eventually became a staunch Methodist. He was converted through the pious example of a beautiful young nun who had visited him while he was in prison in France: 'I have thought then . . . that if I am faithful until death, and she continued in the same way, that she and me shall meet at God's right hand, where we shall sing louder and sweeter than ever I sang in that garden.' Even while still engaged in smuggling, Harry Carter would allow no swearing or 'unseemly conversation' on board his ship, and after his conversion he became a popular preacher – on one occasion, after preaching to a group of smugglers, he noted that 'the men took their hats off, all very serious, no laffing, no trifling conversations'.

Smugglers in those days never considered that this type of religious fervour and honesty coupled with illegal importation was a strange combination: even Lord Holland stated in the House of Lords in 1805 that smuggling was a 'crime which, whatever laws may be made to constitute it a high offence, the mind of man can never conceive as at all equalling in turpitude those acts which are breaches of clear moral virtues'.

Harry Carter's life story, *The Autobiography of a Cornish Smuggler,* reads more like a religious tract than the adventurous narrative one would expect, though we do learn that the Carter family started in the business at an early age and were so successful that they could soon afford to have several cutters built for them. He also tells us that they were imprisoned several times in France though he himself had a narrow escape once when his ship was attacked by two men-of-war. In the fight that ensued, he was left for dead: 'the bone of my nose cut right in two, nothing but a bit of skin holding it, and two very large cuts on my head, that two or three pieces of my skull worked out afterwards'. By some miracle, he managed to slip over the side and stagger to the shore, where he was eventually found and revived by his friends. Soon after this daunting experience, he retired from the trade, and while his brothers continued smuggling, Harry settled down on a small farm in 1789.

At Sennen it is said that the famous First and Last Inn with its unique signboard was the haunt of smugglers and wreckers, led for some sixty years by an intrepid and notorious landlady, one Anne Treave and her trusted lieutenant, the parson!

Smuggling at Penzance was carried out so openly that it was even immortalised by Gilbert and Sullivan in their opera, *The Pirates of Penzance*. Here, everyone took part in it; a customs officer in 1769 mentions that: 'The Mayor of Penzance has always paid for fire and candles for the guardroom but the present Mayor refuses to do so. At this I do not wonder, as he is at present bound over in a large sum not to be again guilty of smuggling.' This was not unusual, for if fair-trading was to work efficiently the whole town had to be in league together, for, although the fishermen and labourers actually handled the goods, the original capital was usually provided by a rich and respectable 'backer'.

Penzance, being one of the most important towns in Cornwall at the time, possessed quite an efficient customs service and the books kept by the officers give a good idea of the extent and nature of the local smuggling operations. In 1775 it was recorded that: 'Two Irish wherries full of men and guns . . . came to anchor within the limits of this port and lay there three days, in open defiance discharging their contraband goods. We are totally destitute of any force to attack them by sea, and as the whole coast is principally inhabited by a lot of smugglers under the denomination of fishermen, it is next to an impossibility to intercept any of these goods after they are landed.'

An even more illuminating record dates from 1778, when two officers went to search a house: 'They obtained from me a search-warrant but were forcibly hindered from executing it by four men, one armed with a pistol and a large whip, the others with sticks and bludgeons. They were told that if they persisted they

Print of St Ives

would have their brains blown out. As the law now stands, I fear a criminal prosecution would have been useless for the reason which it shocks me to mention – that a Cornish jury would certainly acquit the smugglers.'

Penzance customs officers undoubtedly had a hard time carrying out their duties for, while they were risking their lives to make an arrest, the magistrates were simply letting the smugglers go free again. On one occasion, customs officers were threatened by smugglers who 'endeavoured to knock out their brains with a boat-hook, besides throwing large stones at them; in 1772 one of the customs boats was sabotaged and sunk; while one of the most memorable incidents occurred when two excisemen, having received information that a certain James Rogers (a well-known smuggler) was harbouring contraband goods, went to search his house. However, Rogers was waiting for them and attacked them viciously, leaving them horribly injured; he then had the audacity to issue a summons against the unfortunate officers for entering his house without a search-warrant!

The harbour at Mousehole

Previous page: *A brush with smugglers* by Bernard F. Gribble
Left: nineteenth-century fishing boats, Padstow
Below: Padstow harbour
Right: Jamaica Inn

At the nearby harbour of Mousehole smuggling was just as prevalent but the customs officials were rather less willing to risk their lives in the course of duty when the only reward that they could expect was prosecution! They preferred to stay safely out of sight when the smugglers were engaged in a 'run', even though many of these took place in broad daylight. It is, therefore, hardly surprising that, in 1780, all the customs officers stationed at Mousehole were charged not only with accepting bribes from the smugglers, but also with actively assisting these local 'fair-traders' in their illegal escapades!

St Ives once concentrated on the smuggling of luxury goods, and John Knill, Collector of Customs, who was elected Mayor of St Ives in 1767, was believed to be the ringleader of the St Ives smugglers. He was certainly a regular customer at the George and Dragon which was chief among the many smugglers' inns here. 'The George was known for a respectable, high-class church-and-state establishment with no nonsense about it', yet on one occasion its respectable patrons felt no qualms over knocking a revenue officer unconscious to prevent him seeing the train of mules carrying brandy past the door! St Ives was probably the last port in Cornwall to continue smuggling on an organised basis.

As one of the main bases of the customs and excise men, Padstow possessed a Collector of Customs, an Inspector of the Water-Guard, a tide-waiter, a landing-waiter and an officer of excise; all of whom tried in vain to quash illegal trading. But, since they had to watch the surrounding coastline as well as the harbour, Padstow's smuggling operations carried on virtually undisturbed. Indeed, in 1693, a Collector was dismissed for accepting bribes – a common enough event – while once the excise boat, 'Instead of chasing, had been chased into the port by a large Irish vessel which, by way of bravado, fired seven guns at the mouth of the harbour and hung out a flag by way of triumph, and then sailed to Newquay, where smugglers and excise officers were on excellent terms, to discharge her cargo.' William Rawlings truth-fully lamented: 'If in this little spot so much dirty work be done, how much more through the county.' Padstow was also subjected to a little piracy, and one of these local pirate/smugglers was a Captain Piers, whose mother was reported to be a witch. When she was seen

Batt's Close Cottage, showing the bottle-end set in its wall which identified it as a house where the owners would be kindly disposed towards smugglers

on the quay helping to unload the spoils, nobody dared interfere!

Padstow smugglers were certainly ingenious – once, when the excisemen were planning to raid a farmhouse, all the contraband goods were stored in the bedroom, and the farmer's wife, who was pregnant, retired to bed. The doctor was summoned and: 'He at once took charge of the bedroom, into which he forbade the excisemen to enter, on account of the critical condition of his patient. . . . Exactly how much of the contraband the doctor received for the part he had played is unknown!'

The beach at Seaton

On another occasion, an exciseman noticed a farmer carrying a keg of brandy along a winding lane. The farmer just had time to pull a gate post out of its socket, drop the cask in and replace the post before the exciseman caught him up. Naturally, the baffled officer found nothing!

A particularly cunning local trick involved the smugglers' mules. Not only were these hardy beasts sometimes shaved and covered with grease so that they could not be easily caught hold of; but they were also taught the usual words of command in reverse – thus, if a smuggler was ordered to stop, he would obediently shout out 'Whoa!' and the well-trained mule would take off at full speed!

Mules or horses were, of course, quite invaluable for distributing the goods efficiently and quickly. In 1765 William Rawlings described how his servants 'set out some time before day, but by fine moonlight, when, crossing the common, about three miles from us, they met sixty horses, having each three bags of tea on them of fifty-six or fifty-eight pounds weight. All this was landed on a beach about two miles to the west of Padstow and carried from thence through this county and into Devon.'

The most common destinations were inns, where goods could be sampled, stored and, of course, sold; and the best-known smugglers' inn in Cornwall must be Jamaica Inn on the Bodmin road, immortalised by Daphne du Maurier. Goods that found their way to this secluded spot came mainly from Polperro and the little village of Boscastle.

SMUGGLER'S HAUNTS IN DEVON

Landing a cargo by Ibbertson

Smuggling in Devon was really very similar in its methods to that in Cornwall, though there were, of course, a few minor differences. For instance, in Devon the cottages sometimes had a few glass bottle-ends cemented into their walls, just below the eaves. This signified that smugglers would always find a welcome and a helping hand from the owners. The photograph opposite (top) shows one of the bottle-ends that are still to be seen in the walls of the picturesque Batt's Close Cottage, situated on the road from Axminster to Honiton. Once, a narrow and tortuous smugglers' path led from the cottage to Seaton so that they could bring their goods straight here from the beach, with little danger of being apprehended.

Seaton, overhung by rugged cliffs, was another notorious smugglers' resort and was often used as a landing place by Sam Mutter, a celebrated Devonshire smuggler who was a colleague of Jack Rattenbury's. While smuggling may seem, in retrospect, a romantic and colourful profession, in reality there was also a darker side to it and we are reminded of this by an epitaph in Seaton church commemorating William Henry Paulson, 'Who with eight Seamen all Volunteers Perished in a Gale of Wind off Sidmouth Whilst cruising in a Galley for the prevention of Smuggling on the 13th June 1817 in the 23rd Year of his Age.'

Tradition has it that four important parishes played a big part in the essential organisation of smuggling off the coast of South Devon, namely that 'Sidbury financed, Branscombe landed, Sidmouth found wagons and Salcombe carriers'. One dark and stormy night in 1755, a cargo of contraband was expected between Seaton and Beer. The smugglers waiting on land lit a fire to guide the lugger captain in; this was seen by a Preventive Officer named John Hurley, who with the men went down to the shore and attempted to put the fire out. In doing so he fell over the cliff-edge and was killed. His memorial in Branscombe churchyard is a masterpiece, the final words being, 'He was an active and Diligent Officer And very inoffensive in his life and Conversation.'

Since smuggling was never thought of as a crime but rather as a natural way of life, it comes as little surprise to find the Church heavily implicated. The vicarage, being the focal point of village life as well as usually having secret passages, seemed the obvious place from which to regulate operations, while the church itself offered many hiding places for contraband. It could be stored under the pews or even in the pulpit. The parsons generally turned a blind eye to these goings-on while some, such as the eighteenth-century Devon vicars Matt Mundy and Ambrose Stapleton, even played an active part in the proceedings. Coffins full of contraband

Top: the Mount Pleasant Inn, near Dawlish Warren
Above: the Combe Cellars Inn, by the River Teign
Right: the beach at Dawlish Warren
Inset: the church of St Winifred, at Branscombe

could be safely buried in churchyards such as that at the church of St Winifred in Branscombe. Here is an interesting epitaph to 'Mr John Harley, Custom House Officer of this parish', who was killed in the course of duty. Dawlish Warren was also used frequently as a hiding-place, for with its two-mile stretch of sand it was an ideal spot to bury casks.

Inns also played an important part in smuggling, for they provided a ready market for the contraband as well as cellars for storage. They were, of course, a good meeting-place for the discussion of plans, although this could sometimes be a disadvantage if a customs man was eavesdropping! Two such Devon inns were the Mount Pleasant and the Combe Cellars. The Mount Pleasant Inn stands conveniently near Dawlish Warren and from here the fair-traders could signal to their vessels in the bay, while the landlord provided artificial caves in the nearby sandstone rocks. The Combe Cellars Inn lies on the banks of the River Teign, so goods could be easily transported here – this inn could provide storage space for seven tons of tobacco.

The great port of Brixham, further along the coast, was a breeding ground for smugglers, and an amusing story is told of one 'Resurrection' Jackman who was especially adept at evading the revenue men. However, they finally caught up with him at his house, only to find the family in mourning because he had died. Mock funerals were often staged by smugglers so the revenue men were naturally suspicious and set out to follow Jackman's cortège. To their horror, they suddenly realised that the 'corpse' had crept up behind them – they immediately fled, leaving the coffinful of brandy to continue safely on its way.

A similar incident also occurred near Brixham, when a smugglers' look-out man succeeded in frightening away the coastguard by draping himself in his white nightshirt – the appearance of this ghastly apparition, who remarked pleasantly: ''Tis a fine night for the dead to walk,' proved too much for the coastguard!

Yet another character associated with Brixham was Jack Rattenbury, one of the most dashing figures in the annals of smuggling. Once known as the 'Rob Roy of the West', Jack was born in the village of Beer. His father had been taken by the press-gang, so when Jack was nine he was employed on his uncle's fishing boat, but his early seafaring life came to an abrupt end after he lost the rudder! After this disgrace, he moved to Brixham and then returned to Beer to join his uncle on a voyage of piracy. Unfortunately, they were captured by a French ship and were thrown into prison in France. Jack managed to escape and arrived back in Devon more than a year later.

His life from then on was one long adventure, moving from ship to ship till he took up smuggling full time. He usually landed his cargoes at Beer or Brixham, and although he was frequently arrested he always managed to escape, and once he held off some officers of the South Devon Militia with a reaphook. Rattenbury led

Top: Jack Rattenbury
Left: the harbour at Brixham

his last expedition in 1836, when he was nearly sixty, but his son carried on the business almost as successfully.

A more ominous figure was 'Cruel' Coppinger the Dane, a partly fictional character who made his first appearance, off Hartland Point, during a terrible storm. His vessel was wrecked and all were drowned apart from Coppinger – 'With stalwart arm and powerful chest he made his way through the surf, rode manfully from billow to billow, until with a mighty bound he stood at last upright upon the sand, a fine stately semblance of one of the old Vikings of the northern seas. A crowd of people had gathered . . . into their midst and to their astonished dismay rushed the dripping stranger: he snatched from a terrified old dame her red Welsh cloak, cast it loosely around him, and bounded suddenly upon the crupper of a young damsel' (Dinah Hamlyn). Dinah's family welcomed him and he eventually married her, but, 'Immediately afterwards, his evil nature, so long

Top left: Bigbury Bay
Top centre: the Pilchard Inn, Burgh Island
Top right: Hartland Quay, near Hartland Point
Left: Clovelly
Below: 'Cruel' Coppinger

smouldering, broke out like a wild beast uncaged. All at once the house became the den and refuge of every lawless character on the coast. It was discovered that an organised band of desperadoes, smugglers, wreckers and poachers were embarked in a system of bold adventure, and that "Cruel" Coppinger was their Captain.'

He certainly deserved his nickname (given to him by R. S. Hawker, who narrated this tale), for he thought nothing of chopping off the head of an exciseman, while his son, a deaf-mute, once threw a neighbour's boy over a cliff for fun! Coppinger's downfall finally came, how-

ever, and once again the strange ship arrived at Hartland Point. Then, 'He and his boat's crew boarded the vessel, and she was out of sight in a moment, like a spectre or a ghost. Thunder, lightning and hail ensued. Trees were rent up by the roots around the pirate's abode, and, strange to say, a meteoric stone, called in that country a storm-bolt, fell through the roof into the room at the very feet of "Cruel" Coppinger's vacant chair.'

Fortunately, Coppinger was an exception, for the majority of smugglers in the vicinity were more peaceable. Situated on Burgh Island, just off the coast at

Bigbury Bay, is the Pilchard Inn. This was originally built as a rest-house for the pilgrims who came to visit a chapel here, but it soon threw off its early religious associations and became the headquarters of Tom Crocker, an Elizabethan pirate and smuggler. Mention must also be made of Clovelly, described by Charles Dickens as 'A mighty sing'lar and pretty place it is, as ever I saw in all the days of my life.' (From 'A Message from the Sea'.) Yet, despite its beauty and its calm atmosphere nowadays, the old caves once used by gangs of smugglers can still be seen in the Hobby Woods.

Appledore, near Bideford, was once the home of Mr Thomas Benson, a rich and ostensibly respectable merchant who was also the Member of Parliament for Barnstaple. He had a more sinister side to his nature, however, which came to light when he rented Lundy Island. This rocky outcrop, some fifteen miles from the mainland, had suffered a long history of piracy since the reign of Henry II, and during the sixteenth century it was attacked and plundered by a succession of pirates: Turkish, Spanish and French. Benson was both a pirate and a smuggler. He established himself on the island in the now-ruined Marisco Castle, beneath which is a vast grotto where he could hide his spoils. His greatest success came when, in his capacity as a Member of Parliament, he was put in charge of transporting convicts to America. Benson, however, kept their passage money for himself and simply transported them all to Lundy, where he employed them in his smuggling organisation. He was finally discredited and forced to flee.

The Valley of the Rocks, further around the mainland, has a wild and rather eerie landscape which sheers precipitously down to the sea. Now it is only populated by mountain goats, but once it concealed a den of smugglers who found it convenient because very few outsiders were brave enough to venture near (this was partly due to the reputation of Mother Meldrum, the resident witch). When one coastguard did try to capture a smuggler in the valley, the result was tragic, for, in the ensuing fight, both men plunged to their deaths over the cliff tops. Nearby is the secluded Lee Bay which is pockmarked with smugglers' caves and paths – some of these led directly to Countisbury Foreland, from where the goods could be carried along an old pack-horse path into Somerset.

R. D. Blackmore, in his famous romance, *Lorna Doone*, describes how the smugglers 'Land their goods without regard to the King's Revenue at the little haven of Lynmouth'. Today, one of the most picturesque sights in Lynmouth, which nestles below the forbidding cliffs of the Valley of the Rocks, is this little row of thatched cottages, known as Mars Hill. Nothing could seem more innocent, yet every one of these was once involved in smuggling. The cottages were originally built as salting-houses for the fisheries so they had ample storage room, and they were fitted with heavy oak draw-bars so that the doors could be barricaded against unwelcome visitors. The cottage at the top of the row was once the home of the poet Shelley, while at the foot of the hill is the Rising Sun Inn, where the smugglers could meet to collect their goods before transferring them to the donkeys that were waiting patiently outside.

Left: Lynmouth
Inset left: the Valley of the Rocks
Inset centre: Countisbury Foreland
Inset right: Mars Hill, Lynmouth

SMUGGLING METHODS

The great era of West Country smuggling can be roughly divided into two periods, 'Free Trade' and 'Scientific', and the methods used in each differ drastically. The 'Free Trade' period, as its name implies, was really the Golden Age of the smuggler, when there were so few restrictions that the smuggler could, and frequently did, make his fortune with little fear of punishment. While a preventive system did exist, its officers were hopelessly overworked, treated very badly (many had to stand on cliffs in freezing rain all night), invariably outnumbered by smugglers if they did attempt to make an arrest, and were so poorly paid that they usually preferred to accept a bribe than to risk their lives in the course of duty.

One of R. S. Hawker's anecdotes shows how bribery was sometimes arranged – a bag of money was dropped into a hollow in a certain rock for the exciseman and 'there he would go if so be he was a reasonable officer, and the byeword used to be, when 'twas all right, one of us would go and meet him, and then say, "Sir, your pocket is unbuttoned," and he would smile and answer "Ay! ay!, but never mind, my man, my money's safe enough," and thereby we knew that he was a just man, and satisfied, and that the boats could take the roller in peace.'

Even when the customs restrictions were tightened elsewhere in England, they did not penetrate into the West Country. During this period then, the goods, which were bought in France and Brittany, were landed openly on the beach where they were met by crowds of local people, some of whom were known as batmen and

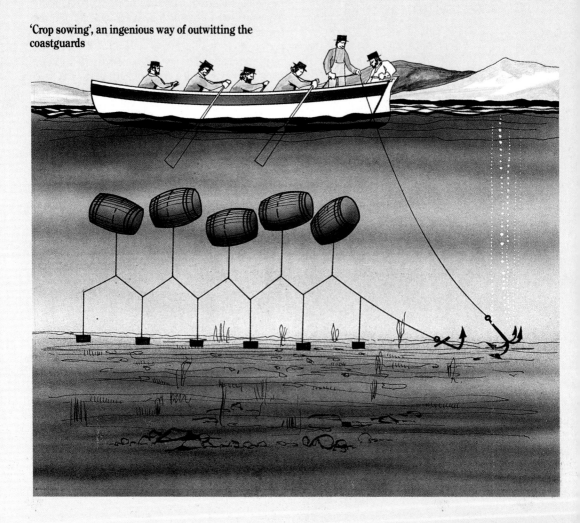

'Crop sowing', an ingenious way of outwitting the coastguards

were armed with cudgels just in case there were any interruptions. The rest of the men wore a special harness which enabled them to carry two tubs of spirits each; these tubs were flat so that they could be more easily transported. Horses were also 'borrowed' from farmers if an especially heavy cargo was expected, and it would then be efficiently and quickly distributed to the numerous hiding-places in houses and inns where goods could be stored till they were needed.

At this time, smuggling was a comradely affair, with generous rewards given to all the participants. When the train of men and horses had to pass through a village, the inhabitants would turn their faces to the wall so that they could truthfully say that they had seen nothing if they were questioned by the revenue men – in the words of a poem by Rudyard Kipling, 'Watch the wall, my darling, while the gentlemen go by.' Once the goods arrived at their destination they ceased to be illegal because, until the laws were changed in the nineteenth century, the actual selling of contraband was not an offence.

The times were changing, however, for when the war against France ended in 1815 the Government suddenly had enough surplus men and ships as well as enough time and money to form a more efficient preventive service. This was the beginning of the 'Scientific' Period, for smuggling was too essential and lucrative a way of life to be relinquished at the first sign of trouble, so, when the revenue officers became an organised force, the smugglers realised that they had to follow suit if they were to survive. They could no longer rely on the old-fashioned landings but they were, with a few exceptions, loath to use violence unless it was absolutely necessary. Thus, they began to devise some ingenious methods of outwitting the coastguard.

The earliest of these was 'crop-sowing'. The smuggling boats would anchor some way off shore and the 'ankers' (tubs) would be fastened to a length of rope, interspersed with heavy stones with an anchor at either end. Then, under cover of darkness, the tubs would be dropped overboard at a pre-arranged spot. Later, innocent-looking fishing boats would casually halt over the spot and, using special pronged hooks known as 'creepers' or 'centipedes', they would draw up the tubs and conceal them under their nets. These tubs could then be buried in the sand until they could be safely collected. The coastguards, not wanting to be outdone (they could earn 'prize-money' for each captured cargo), spent much of their time 'creeping' in likely spots hoping

Below left: false-sided water tank used to conceal spirits
Below right: a special harness to enable two tubs of spirits to be carried at once
Bottom: cross-section of a boat, showing how a false bottom could be constructed in order to hide contraband

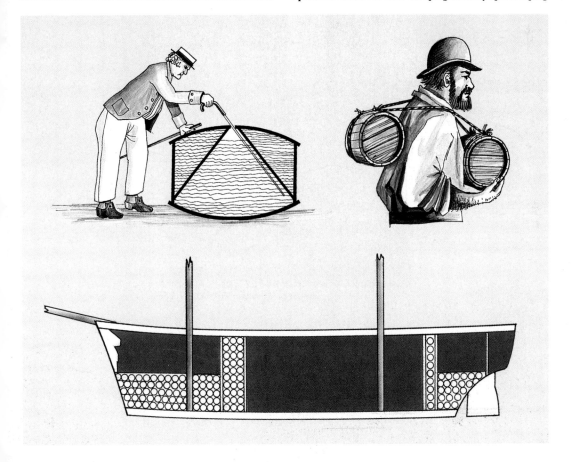

to find contraband before the smugglers could lift it. The smugglers employed 'flashers' who signalled from the shore when the coast was clear (they used a special lantern with a long funnel so that the light could only be seen from one direction), but occasionally the tubs were submerged for so long before they could be recovered that the contents became sour and vile-smelling, in which case they were known as 'stinkibus'.

While crop-sowing was always the most popular method, the coastguards became too proficient at 'creeping', and although the smugglers were usually quite content if they could recover one cargo out of three, they began to experiment with more sophisticated methods. They came to the conclusion that it would be simpler to hide the goods on the actual boats, so boats with ingenious false bottoms became a common requirement. The cargo could also be disguised as ballast; tobacco was plaited inside the many ropes used on board ship, and spirits could be hidden inside a water-tank with false sides. One captain created a false ceiling in his cabin, while another stuffed a turkey with rare silks – it is hardly surprising that the preventive force were frequently baffled. When a ship was discovered to be concealing contraband, however, it was sawn up into three parts, thus ruining many a smuggler's business completely.

Although bribery was still in evidence, the preventive force was growing stronger and more loyal all the time, and it was this factor, coupled with a reduction of customs duties on goods, that finally led to the decline in smuggling throughout Devon and Cornwall. Smuggling was simply no longer viable, for the risks had increased dramatically while the profits were now only marginal. Thus, though individuals continued to bring contraband into the country, the great era of organised smuggling was at last a thing of the past.